D0929467

07 13 13 SAT

Shakira

Shakira

Other books in the People in the News series:

Shakira

by Holly Day

LUCENT BOOKS

An imprint of Thomson Gale, a part of The Thomson Corporation

Detroit • New York • San Francisco • New Haven, Conn. • Waterville, Maine • London

For Sherman, with all my love

© 2007 Thomson Gale, a part of The Thomson Corporation.

Thomson and Star Logo are trademarks and Gale and Lucent Books are registered trademarks used herein under license.

For more information, contact:
Lucent Books
27500 Drake Rd.
Farmington Hills, MI 48331-3535
Or you can visit our Internet site at http://www.gale.com

ALL RIGHTS RESERVED.
No part of this work covered by the copyright hereon may be reproduced or used in any form or by any means—graphic, electronic, or mechanical, including photocopying, recording, taping, Web distribution or information storage retrieval systems—without the written permission of the publisher.

Every effort has been made to trace the owners of copyrighted material.

LIBRARY OF CONGRESS CATALOGING-IN-PUBLICATION DATA

Day, Holly.
  Shakira / by Holly Day.
    p. cm. — (People in the news)
  Includes bibliographical references (p.) and index.
  ISBN-13: 978-1-59018-974-0 (hardcover)
  1. Shakira—Juvenile literature. 2. Singers—Latin America—Biography—Juvenile
literature. I. Title.
  ML3930.S46D39 2007
  782.42164092—dc22
  [B]
                                                     2007007025

ISBN-10: 1-59018-974-4

Printed in the United States of America

Contents

F ame and celebrity are alluring. People are drawn to those who walk in fame's spotlight, whether they are known for great accomplishments or for notorious deeds. The lives of the famous pique public interest and attract attention, perhaps because their experiences seem in some ways so different from, yet in other ways so similar to, our own.

Newspapers, magazines, and television regularly capitalize on this fascination with celebrity by running profiles of famous people. For example, television programs such as *Entertainment Tonight* devote all of their programming to stories about entertainment and entertainers. Magazines such as *People* fill their pages with stories of the private lives of famous people. Even newspapers, newsmagazines, and television news frequently delve into the lives of well-known personalities. Despite the number of articles and programs, few provide more than a superficial glimpse at their subjects.

Lucent's People in the News series offers young readers a deeper look into the lives of today's newsmakers, the influences that have shaped them, and the impact they have had in their fields of endeavor and on other people's lives. The subjects of the series hail from many disciplines and walks of life. They include authors, musicians, athletes, political leaders, entertainers, entrepreneurs, and others who have made a mark on modern life and who, in many cases, will continue to do so for years to come.

These biographies are more than factual chronicles. Each book emphasizes the contributions, accomplishments, or deeds that have brought fame or notoriety to the individual and shows how that person has influenced modern life. Authors portray their subjects in a realistic, unsentimental light. For example, Bill Gates—the cofounder and chief executive officer of the software giant Microsoft—has been instrumental in making personal computers the most vital tool of the modern age. Few dispute his business savvy, his perseverance, or his technical expertise, yet critics say he is ruthless in his dealings with competitors and driven more by his desire to maintain Microsoft's dominance in the computer industry than by an interest in furthering technology.

In these books, young readers will encounter inspiring stories about real people who achieved success despite enormous obstacles. Oprah Winfrey—the most powerful, most watched, and wealthiest woman on television today—spent the first six years of her life in the care of her grandparents while her unwed mother sought work and a better life elsewhere. Her adolescence was colored by promiscuity, pregnancy at age fourteen, rape, and sexual abuse.

Each author documents and supports his or her work with an array of primary and secondary source quotations taken from diaries, letters, speeches, and interviews. All quotes are footnoted to show readers exactly how and where biographers derive their information and provide guidance for further research. The quotations enliven the text by giving readers eyewitness views of the life and accomplishments of each person covered in the People in the News series.

In addition, each book in the series includes photographs, annotated bibliographies, timelines, and comprehensive indexes. For both the casual reader and the student researcher, the People in the News series offers insight into the lives of today's newsmakers—people who shape the way we live, work, and play in the modern age.

The Lioness of the Stage

E ven as a small child, Shakira loved to perform in front of people. At the tender age of four, she astonished family members and friends with an impromptu belly dance that was as good as the performance of the professional belly dancers of the restaurant where they dined. She was sitting in a Middle Eastern restaurant in her hometown of Barranquilla, Colombia, listening to the sound of the *doumbek*, the drum that traditionally accompanies belly dancing. One of the dancers picked the little girl out of the roomful of diners and taught her a few belly dancing moves.

Years later, women around the world would be inspired to take up belly dancing solely because they had seen an adult Shakira do it onstage or on TV. This is just one example of Shakira's wide-ranging influence on popular culture.

The Beginning

From that point on, Shakira was belly dancing everywhere—in her bedroom, in the park, at family gatherings, and even in front of the nuns at her convent school. The little girl from the city of Barranquilla was building up her fan base before she had even decided what kind of star she was going to be.

When Shakira was eight, her attention shifted from dancing to writing. She began writing poetry, stories, and song lyrics, typing away at the big, bulky typewriter she had asked for as a

Christmas gift. A little while later, an aunt gave her a guitar, and Shakira began combining her poetry with music.

Soon, Shakira was performing her songs at local events and even toured with a small children's troupe around Colombia. Her parents fully supported her dreams of becoming a star, and her mother began taking Shakira to TV show auditions to see if she could help her daughter gain more than just local exposure.

Shakira took up belly dancing at an early age. Her first performance took place at a restaurant where professional belly dancers taught her some moves.

A Rising Star

When she was thirteen, a record label executive at Sony Columbia offered her a recording contract for her next three albums. While her first two albums, *Magia* (Magic) and *Peligro* (Danger), received some attention on the local level, it was not until her third album, *Pies Descalzos* (Bare Feet), that people outside of Colombia began to take notice of Shakira. As her album began to creep up the Latin charts in the United States, Shakira found her confidence in her musical instincts growing as well. With her friend Emilio Estefan Jr. helping guide her in the studio, Shakira began to learn how to produce her own records, giving her even more control of the finished product.

A New World

While it is possible for a Spanish-speaking star to make an impact on the U.S. charts, it is easier for that star to do so if they speak English. Shakira took two years off from music to work with a tutor and learn how to do just that, as she did not want to have to rely on another person—not even her close friend and mentor, Gloria Estefan—to translate her work for her.

Her first English-language album, *Laundry Service*, proved that Shakira would indeed have crossover success. Shakira soon moved to the United States with her fiancé, Antonio de la Rúa, to live in Miami Beach. Her parents also moved from Colombia to be close to Shakira, as did her brother and lifetime personal manager, Tonino.

World Impact

In 2003 Shakira was named the youngest Goodwill Ambassador by UNICEF. She had been working with homeless children in Colombia for years under her own foundation, Pies Descalzos. As a UNICEF ambassador, Shakira went to poverty-stricken places throughout the world, bringing information about the living con-

*Shakira poses with children at her Pies Descalzos (Bare Feet)
Foundation in Quibdó, Colombia.*

ditions of those regions' poorest children back to the UN and the
world.

Throughout her career, Shakira has proven herself willing to
be courageous enough, strong enough, and stubborn enough to
face up to almost any problem that has come her way. When
those close to her suggested it might be safer for her to end her
relationship with de la Rúa when his father, the president of
Argentina, was removed from power, she stuck by her fiancé and
moved with him to the United States. When record company

executives suggested she make changes to her albums, she almost always stuck by her original musical concept. When publicists suggested that her overt political statements might alienate mainstream audiences, she stood by her ideals, claiming that pop music was meant to be controversial. She has learned through trial and error that the most important decisions in her life have to be made by her, and she has continued to make a huge impact on the world of pop music by trusting in her own good instincts.

Chapter 1

An Early Start

Shakira Isabel Mebarak Ripoll was born on Wednesday, February 2, 1977, in the Clinica Asuncion in Barranquilla, Colombia. Shakira's father, William Mebarak Chadid, was born in New York City after his own parents had emigrated from Lebanon. They then moved to Barranquilla while he was still a child. Shakira's mother, Nidia del Carmen Ripoll Torado, was a native Barranquillian of Catalan-Colombian descent.

When Nidia first met William, she thought he looked like Omar Sharif, a famous actor of that day. This was apparently quite a coincidence, since Nidia had allegedly prayed to meet a man who looked like Sharif the night before. William was a professional jeweler who wrote poetry and short stories in his spare time. As an adult, he had taken over his family's jewelry business and managed to make a good living for himself and his first wife in Barranquilla.

When Nidia and William married, he was divorced and already had nine children from his previous marriage. In naming her daughter, Nidia had shuffled through several names containing the letter k to go well with the sound of the k in Mebarak. She had originally considered Karime and Katiuska, but finally chose Shakira, an Arabic name derived from the word *shukram* (or *shokran*), which means "woman full of grace," or "grateful."

Little Shakira, fondly nicknamed "Cachita" or "Shaki" by her family, was Nidia and William's only child together, but since her older half-siblings lived just a few blocks away, she spent

Shakira has always been very close to her family. She is shown here with her parents.

almost as much time with them as if they all lived in the same house. In many ways, she had the best of both worlds—she got to see what it was like to be an only child, with her own bedroom and her parents' undivided attention, but she also got to have the enviable position of being the youngest child in a large family. She was often doted on by her three older half-sisters, Lucy, Ana, and Patricia, and five half-brothers, Alberto, Edward, Moises, Tonino, and Robin. Today, when Shakira talks about her family, she never uses "half" when talking about her siblings.

A Precocious Child

The Mebaraks were a middle-class family and kept a nice house in the neighborhood of El Limoncito, located in the northern part of Barranquilla. Shakira grew up in a house full of books and music. Her father spent most of his free time sitting at the type-writer, writing and listening to traditional Arabic and American 1970s and 1980s pop music.

Nidia read to her daughter as often as she could, filling the little girl's head with everything from the classics to daily readings from the Bible. According to Nidia, Shakira knew the alphabet by the time she was eighteen months old, and by the time she was three, she knew how to write her own name and read children's books. Shakira's favorite book was Robert Louis Stevenson's *Treasure Island*—a fitting first book for a child living so close to the Caribbean Sea.

By the time Shakira was four years old, her mother felt she was ready for school. Nidia believed Shakira was a child prodigy and claimed she was even composing poetry by then. She had her daughter tested academically, and even though Shakira was considered too young and too small to be allowed to attend regular school, she was admitted into the preschool program at La

Enseñanza de Barranquilla (the Education of Barranquilla)—one of the most prestigious institutions in the city.

La Enseñanza was an all-girl Catholic school run by missionary nuns from the Order of Mary. The nuns were as determined to teach their young charges to be little ladies as they were to teach them reading, writing, and arithmetic. Soon after starting school, little Shakira, nicknamed "Enana," or "dwarf," by her classmates, began belly dancing for her classmates and teachers every Friday in a civic show held by the school. "Even though I danced in the custom of showing the belly, the nuns considered it a dance and an art,"[1] says Shakira.

When Shakira was in second grade, she tried to join the school choir, only to be told by the choir teacher that her vibrato was too strong. Shakira's classmates told her that her voice sounded like the bleating of a goat, and the teacher agreed, stating that her voice was throwing the rest of the singers off key. Shakira took the matter to heart, and it depressed her greatly. Her whole life, she had been surrounded by people who had praised, encouraged, and loved her, and to have someone she had wanted so badly to impress criticize her was devastating. At home, Shakira's parents consoled her as best they could and urged her to forget what the teacher had said. Luckily, Shakira was a determined child, and after some reflection, she decided that she was not going to let the choir teacher's rejection keep her from doing what she loved.

Still, the incident kept her from wanting to sing in public for a while. She began to write lyrics for songs in secret, performing them only for her family and close friends.

Early Ambition

When Shakira was eight, she wrote her first true song, "Tus Gafas Oscuras" (Your Dark Glasses), which commemorated a defining moment in Shakira's otherwise idyllic childhood. When Shakira was two years old, her older brother, whom she had never actually met, was killed by a drunk driver. Shakira's father was completely devastated. However, as the father of many other children,

A Seaside Paradise

Located on the coast of the warm, gentle waters of the Caribbean Sea, Barranquilla has been a popular stop for seafaring merchants and tourists since the Spanish discovered it in the seventeenth century. It was once known as La Puerta de Oro de Colombia, or Colombia's Golden Gate, by the Spanish traders that docked their ships there. The city is still the most important seaport in Colombia, importing and exporting tons of coffee and petroleum each year.

Barranquilla is home to the second-largest Carnival celebrations in South America, with only Brazil's Rio de Janeiro Carnival being the largest. The Carnival in Barranquilla is a celebration with traditions dating back to the nineteenth century, and it was recently proclaimed by UNESCO (United Nations Educational, Scientific and Cultural Organization) to be a Masterpiece of the Oral and Intangible Heritage of Humanity. During Carnival, Barranquilla's normal activities are almost completely suspended, replaced instead by street dances, live music, and parades filled with fantastically costumed performers.

Barranquilla is lovingly known as Curramba la Bella (Curramba the Beautiful), and those hailing from Barranquilla are known as Curramberos. The word for a woman from Barranquilla is *Barranquillera,* while a man is a *Barranquillero.*

The second-largest Carnival celebration in South America takes place in Barranquilla.

especially a very small one, he was determined to keep his grief hidden and be strong for them. To hide his grief, he wore very large, dark sunglasses around his family at all times for nearly a year after the incident.

Little Shakira was almost as frightened by her father wearing sunglasses around at all times—even at night—as she might have been by his grief. Part love song, part fearful question, the poem that became "Tus Gafas Oscuras" was written about this period of her father's life. "I have a phobia of the subject of death," says Shakira. "Death of relationships, death of feelings, physical death, my death, but especially the death of people I love."[2]

The second defining moment came when Shakira was nine. After floundering as an unsuccessful businessman for years, her father lost his jewelry store. Shakira and her parents had to leave their comfortable, middle-class home and move to a cramped apartment in Los Angeles, California, until their finances recovered. Shakira had to leave her school, her friends, and especially her loving siblings behind. "Both things have defined the kind of person I am," she says about these painful memories. "I think all of us spend our childhoods constructing a mandate that is going to drive us through life. Mine was wanting to belong to this family, wanting to generate joy for my parents and make them proud."[3] Perhaps this explains why, when most girls her age were playing with dolls and giggling about boys, Shakira was asking Santa Claus for career-related gifts like typewriters and writing paper. She spent much of her free time shut up in her bedroom, her typewriter rattling out poetry, short stories, and song lyrics at all hours of the day.

Becoming a Star

After "Tus Gafas Oscuras," Shakira began writing more and more songs. She began playing guitar seriously and learned how to put her words to music. While she might have thought that no one was paying much attention to her new obsession, her mother took notice. Nidia went out and found Shakira a voice coach and began actively encouraging her musical career. When Shakira was ten,

Nidia enrolled her in modeling classes at Passarela Academy in Barranquilla. There she learned how to do her own makeup and hair, walk gracefully, and smile for the camera. She took modern dance and movement classes while at Passarela, as well as two years of Olympic gymnastics at Atlantic Coldeportes. Some of her classmates had already started on their own modeling and acting careers, and Shakira was determined to become as successful as they.

At Passarela Academy, Shakira also found the confidence to begin singing in public once more. Shakira's parents began signing her up to compete in singing and dancing competitions around Barranquilla. When Shakira performed in youth competitions, the powerful vibrato voice that had annoyed her choir teacher was as welcome as a breath of fresh air to the contest judges. It was completely original, especially compared to the soft voices of the other elementary school girls and boys in the competitions. By the time she was ten, Shakira had won her first trophy, and within a year, she had won a major award from the television show *Vivan los Niños* (The Children Live), where she competed against other young talents from around the country; the first prize that year was a new bicycle. *Vivan los Niños* was broadcast in several cities via station Telecaribe of Colombia. Shakira ended up winning this particular competition three years in a row, as well as winning the runner-up position in a Niña Atlántico (Atlantic Girl) beauty contest.

The burst of confidence these awards gave her only added to her already competitive nature. She grew to love being onstage and performing for audiences, and people were beginning to take notice of the little girl with the big voice.

Up on the Stage

It soon became obvious that Barranquilla was too small to contain an ambitious little fish like Shakira. When she was ten years old, she joined a local children's troupe and performed across mining towns and villages in Colombia. Her parents

Shakira performs at the TD BankNorth Garden in Boston. Shakira began her career as a child, so she became comfortable with the stage at an early age.

accompanied her wherever she went. She often performed wearing sequined cowgirl outfits and lots of makeup and hair spray. This small competitive circuit formed the foundation of Shakira's career. The constant performing helped Shakira become comfortable with herself onstage. It also enabled her to make her first contacts inside the entertainment industry. Between the ages of ten and thirteen, Shakira was invited to so many music and dance events in and around Barranquilla that she soon found herself becoming a local celebrity. Shakira's parents—especially her mother—were utterly convinced the little girl was destined to be a star.

Their determination and confidence eventually paid off. When Shakira was thirteen, she met local theater producer Monica Ariza. Ariza was so impressed with Shakira that she was determined to help make her known outside Barranquilla. During a flight from Barranquilla to Bogotá, Ariza happened to be sitting next to Sony Columbia record executive Ciro Vargas. She spent much of the plane ride talking to Vargas about her favorite new starlet, Shakira, and by the end of the flight, Vargas agreed to hold an audition for Shakira.

Ariza brought Shakira to meet Vargas a few days later, and Shakira performed an impromptu a cappella (without musical accompaniment) set for Vargas in the hotel lobby. It was a risky move on Shakira's part, but it proved to be worth it. Vargas was utterly won over by the little girl's raw talent. He returned to the Sony office and gave a tape of Shakira's music to the artistic director, raving about the girl's talent. However, the director was not excited at all by the tape or Shakira.

Vargas was convinced that Shakira had talent, and he set up a surprise audition in Colombia's capital city of Bogotá. He tricked the Sony Columbia executives into coming to a bar, and around midnight he announced he had a surprise. As the executives watched, the thirteen-year-old Shakira took the stage and sang three of her original songs. Her performance was a hit. Within a

The Festival Viña del Mar

The Festival Viña del Mar is one of the biggest music festivals in Latin America. It has been held every February since 1970 in the resort city of Viña del Mar, Chile, and is broadcast live on television and radio stations around the world.

The Festival lasts for six days and nights and is held in the Quinta Vergara amphitheater. One musical performer or group from each Latin American country is sent to the festival each year as a representative of that nation, where they compete against each other for the coveted Gaviota de Plata (Silver Seagull) award. After the competition is over, musicians from Chile and from around the world perform for the rest of the festival.

When fifteen-year-old Shakira was sent as Colombia's representative to the festival, she did not come home with the grand prize. However, years later, she returned to the festival to perform—not as a contestant, but as part of a roster of international stars that have included performers like Enrique Iglesias, Jennifer Lopez, the Police, Duran Duran, Ricky Martin, and the Backstreet Boys.

The Festival Viña del Mar is held in the Quinta Vergara amphitheater.

week, Shakira had signed a three-album deal with Sony Discos, the Latin division of Sony Records.

In the Studio

In 1991 a fourteen-year-old Shakira released her debut album, *Magia* (Magic), produced by Miguel E. Cubillos and Pablo Tedeschi. The album was made up of songs she had written over the past five or six years and included some material she had written when she was eight and nine years old. The first single, the title track "Magia," was a song she wrote for her first boyfriend, Óscar Pardo.

The record release party was held in the Teatro Amira de la Rosa, the biggest theater in Barranquilla. Apparently, Sony had high hopes for the album's commercial success and had gone the extra mile to make sure its debut was as memorable as the album itself was supposed to be. *Magia* was originally released in Colombia, but since the album only sold about a thousand copies locally, Sony decided not to release it outside of South America. The album was a success locally but did not have the international appeal that both Sony and Shakira were hoping for, despite releasing a music video for the title track and having had significant radio airtime. It did lead to her being chosen to represent her country at the Festival OTI in Spain, but because she was under the minimum age of sixteen, her participation in the festival was disallowed at the last minute.

Disappointed by the lack of success of her first album, Shakira took a break from music after *Magia* and buried herself in her schoolwork. She sailed through her classes with ease and ended up graduating high school when she was fifteen. Instead of going on to college, however, she decided to head back to the studio and record another album. Her next album was *Peligro*, or Danger. In Shakira's eyes, *Peligro* was a disaster before it even left the studio. Determined to make up for their losses on Shakira's first album, Sony Discos rushed to get the second album out on the street. Shakira lost creative control, and the result was an album that mirrored producer Eduardo Pazz's vision rather than Shakira's. Although the ballad "Tú Seras la Historia de Mi Vida" (You Will Be the History of My Life) was played on local radio stations, and Shakira was invited to represent Colombia in the Festival Viña del Mar with her song "Eres," the album sales were so low that Sony decide not to continue with the third contracted Shakira album. At fifteen, Shakira's recording career seemed to be ending as quickly as it had started.

Chapter 2

Finding Her Voice

Despite the setback in her music career, Shakira was determined to make a name for herself in the entertainment world. She persuaded her mother to allow her to move to Bogotá, thinking that living in the bigger city would provide more opportunities for her. Nidia packed their bags and temporarily moved with Shakira to a modest boardinghouse in Bogotá, while Shakira's father stayed behind in Barranquilla. Once again, Shakira began the arduous process of waiting in cattle call lines to audition for small parts in television shows. It was not long before the seventeen-year-old Shakira landed the role of Luisa María on the daytime Colombian soap opera *El Oasis*. She played a rich girl destined for one ill-fated romance after another. The producers of *El Oasis* also contracted Shakira to sing the show's theme song, "Lo Mío," which was composed by Emilio Estefan.

Best Rear End

Shakira did not find acting very fulfilling, and her lack of enthusiasm most likely was a major factor in her less-than-perfect performances on the show. "I was a very bad actress but I had a lot of fun," admits Shakira. "Besides, someone had to pay the bills."[4] The only honor that came her way was a readers' poll for *TV y Novelas* magazine that named her the winner of the Best Rear End on Television 1994 contest. She stuck with the show, however, and her time on the production was enough to widen both her

Shakira was a big fan of Kurt Cobain.

audience and network of contacts in the entertainment business, including Patricia Téllez, the director of special projects for Caracol Television. Téllez eventually made Shakira the channel's exclusive music artist, which meant that Shakira could be contracted to sing the theme songs for additional television shows besides *El Oasis*.

One good thing about being a television soap actress was that the steady work allowed her more free time to discover the new urban world around her. As a child in Barranquilla, Shakira's main musical influences were whatever her parents happened to be listening to inside the home. Now, as a young woman in a major city, she had access to Top 40 radio stations that played American music, old and new, as well as music from local pop stars. She fell madly in love with American rock music and began using her extra cash to shop at local music stores, buying up all the rock records she could get her hands on. Soon, the music of Tom Petty, Aerosmith, the Clash, and, in particular, Nirvana recordings began filling the tiny apartment she and her mother shared. "I remember the first time I saw Kurt Cobain," she says. "I saw the 'Smells Like Teen Spirit' video and instantly fell in love with him, even though I couldn't see his face. I just wanted to see his face so much. After weeks of finding out anything I could about Nirvana, I saw his face—and he had a face like an angel. I loved him. He was my platonic love."[5] Like the rest of his fans, Shakira was devastated when the troubled star committed suicide, and she could not listen to his music without feeling a sense of loss.

The music Shakira was listening to started to have a huge impact on the music she was writing. She started playing her guitar more and composing songs with a much harder edge than the bubblegum pop songs that had filled her earlier records. A demo tape of her new material found its way into the hands of a local record producer, and soon, the song "¿Dónde Estás Corazón?" (Where Are You, Love?) was featured on a Colombian rock compilation called Nuestro Rock (Our Rock).

Shakira suddenly found herself propelled up the Latin American charts like she never had been with any of her previous releases. It was the first affirmation she had that she should follow her own instincts when it came to making her music. She did not need to fit into any record company executive's idea of what she should sound like.

She reapproached Sony about her unfinished contract, offering that since this was her last album on contract with the label, they should let her put out the kind of record she would actually want to listen to. While it was a hard sell on her part, Sony recognized that since Shakira had been so busy building a name for herself, she was worth the risk. They agreed to give her one last chance. The studio gave her a budget of thirty thousand dollars to record the album—one of the smallest recording allotments Sony had offered to a contracted performer.

Taking the Wheel

This time, Shakira went into the studio knowing exactly what she wanted her album to sound like, as well as the confidence and determination not to let anyone tell her otherwise. When executives at Sony suggested she concentrate on writing what they thought to be more commercially successful music, she politely declined. Instead, she insisted on recording an album of her very own brand of music, a blend of hard-edged guitar rock, pop, and world music that was completely her own.

"I used to have many more difficulties at the beginning of my career," admits Shakira. "When I was 13 years old, I recorded my first album. I was very opinionated and sure about what I wanted, and it was very hard to be part of the adult world and give my opinion every 20 seconds when people wouldn't understand that. Executives just wanted to have control of me and my career."[6]

Shakira describes her fight for control:

It was definitely a battle to be faithful to myself. There was some kind of rule in Latin America: to be able to be a successful singer, you had to use the roots of Latin music. So when they first discovered me, they wanted to make me a merengue singer. I said "What?! Are you nuts?!" I mean, when I go to a disco I'll dance to a couple of merengue songs, but it's certainly not my type of music.[7]

But Shakira learned how to take charge of her career, saying:

Now I tell them, "Please trust me. I have good instincts." And they say, "Yeah, but we have experts." And I say, "I'm

Humble Roots for a Big Star

Like Shakira, Emilio Estefan Jr. had very humble beginnings. In 1968, when he was fifteen years old, he moved from Cuba to a Miami, Florida, apartment with fifteen other family members. He soon found work running errands for the people who ran the beauty contests along the beach, until he was offered a full-time job as a mailroom clerk for Bacardi Company.

While all this was going on, however, Estefan was secretly indulging in his real passion: music. He started a group that became known as the Miami Latin Boys, which had moderate success playing at private parties and events around Miami. He was playing one such event when he met his future wife, Gloria. He asked her to join the group, and the group was renamed the Miami Sound Machine. By the early 1980s, the group had become a major international band, with such songs as "Get on Your Feet" and "Conga" becoming number one hits in many countries. After Gloria Estefan decided to leave the group and embark on a solo career in 1987, Emilio Estefan decided to become a full-time music producer. Since the 1980s, he has produced records for many stars, including his wife, Jennifer Lopez, and Shakira.

an expert too. I know Shakira better than anybody. I know what works for Shakira, because I've already made my mistakes, and I know what path I should follow and which one I shouldn't." For instance, I let them pluck my eyebrows. You know, the time I gave myself up like that, it was the lesson of my life: I have to be really in control.[8]

Learning to take control of her music and career was one of the hardest things Shakira had to learn how to do. However, her determination to stay in control so early in her career made it harder for people to make decisions for her later on.

A New Producer

Shakira knew enough about making records to know that the perfect producer was necessary to make the perfect record. She had decided early on that ultimately, she wanted to be her own perfect producer, but since she did not know much about the technology that rules recording studios, she had to be satisfied with finding a producer she could trust with her music. She enlisted the help of producer and recording engineer Luis Fernando Ochoa to help her in the studio and began to learn how to find her way around a recording studio mixing board.

Ochoa was the perfect adviser to Shakira—he kept his hands off her music and offered advice only when Shakira asked for it. He also helped her round up the backup musicians for the new album by calling on his local music connections, and he even performed on many of the instruments on the record. Ochoa, who was born in the United States and only moved to Colombia after becoming an adult, was almost by nature the perfect choice for producing an album that depended as much on North American music as it did Latin American. He was intimately familiar with the roots of rock music, having grown up around it, but had chosen to immerse himself in the Colombian music scene.

The resulting album, *Pies Descalzos* (Bare Feet), was initially released in Colombia in 1995. The album was a slow seller at first, but thanks to early success of the chart-topping song "Estoy Aquí" (I'm Here), the album was soon a hit all over South America, selling over 1 million copies in Brazil alone. Sony rereleased the album in 1996, and it hit number one in eight different countries and eventually went platinum in the United States as well.

Pies Descalzos was the first real step in establishing Shakira as an international star. Before Shakira, the role of Latin American women in music was traditionally a much more subdued one. Shakira's music and persona aroused controversy from the day

Shakira performs at the 2002 World Music Awards. She was named the Latin Female Artist of the Year at the 1998 World Music Awards.

the new record hit the shelves. Much like female Latin music stars from the United States, such as Selena and Jennifer Lopez, Shakira was determined to be not just another pretty girl singing about how happy she was with her boyfriend. Instead, Shakira's new music concentrated just as much on the flaws of human relation-

Critics compared Shakira to other pop stars like Alanis Morissette.

ships as it did on the good times. Critics compared her to U.S. pop stars like Alanis Morissette and Britney Spears, and her mostly female audiences instantly adored her. She was considered by many to be the voice of the new generation of Latin American women—independent, self-sufficient, and determined to be in control.

The album won *Billboard* magazine's award for best new album in 1997, and Shakira was named the Latin female artist of the year at the 1998 World Music Awards. Working on the record served Ochoa well, too—after working with Shakira, he went on to produce records for many other Latin pop stars, including Ricky Martin and Enrique Iglesias.

Triumph and Tragedy

While Shakira was finding herself more and more comfortable in the recording studio, her first love was still performing for live audiences. Soon after *Pies Descalzos* came out, Shakira was eager to hit the road and promote her new material, and, as usual, her family prepared to join the 1997 tour to support the rising superstar. Along with her parents, her older brother Tonino—now her permanent tour manager—readied himself for what would be a two-year-long tour. The tour would take them to nearly every Spanish-speaking country in the world, as well as cities in the United States with large Hispanic populations.

The tour was not just about music, however. Shakira was quickly becoming an avid student of political and social history, and every country the tour touched down on became a subject of intense scrutiny to the rising star. Her growing stardom was beginning to open doors that Shakira had never dreamed would be unlocked for her. While in Italy, she was granted an audience with Pope John II—something that must have thrilled the very devout Nidia almost as much as it did Shakira. Upon her return home, the government of Colombia made Shakira a Goodwill Ambassador, which meant that now when she went on tour, she was officially representing her home country. The album and tour helped to make Shakira one of the most visible musical performers in Latin music.

At the end of the tour, Shakira returned to Barranquilla for a huge homecoming concert. It was her first concert in her hometown since her first album came out. Nearly fifty thousand fans showed up for the event, and the crowds turned out to be too large for the venue. The crowd went wild when Shakira took the stage, and two young girls were trampled to death in the resulting stampede.

Shakira was deeply affected by the event, taking the incident as a sign from God that perhaps she should quit singing. She ended the tour and sank into a deep depression. "She thought that it was her fault those people had died because they went to see her sing,"[9] said her brother Tonino. Her family and friends did what they could to lift Shakira's spirits again, and eventually, they made her see that the deaths were not her fault and that she should continue her music and her career.

Back in the Studio

By this time, it was obvious that Shakira was meant to be a musician and not an actress. In 1997 she said goodbye to the cast at *El Oasis*, where she was still considered to be an official cast member—even though she had not been on the show as a regular cast member for nearly two years—and began to concentrate full-time on her music career. Since so much of her time had been spent on the road and not in the studio, Sony was worried that Shakira's name would be forgotten if she did not release another record soon. Still buoyed by the faces and countries she had seen on her tour, Shakira went into the studio once more, essentially to rewrite *Pies Descalzos* for another audience— her fans in Brazil. The original album had sold over nine hundred thousand copies in that country alone, and in homage to this huge fan base, *The Remixes* not only featured remixes of the original material, but some of the songs were completely rewritten in Portuguese.

The release of *The Remixes* bought Shakira enough time to head back into the studio and begin working on new material

Gloria and Emilio Estefan Jr. helped provide guidance to Shakira.

without fear of her audience forgetting who she was. While still on the set at *El Oasis*, she had become acquainted with producer and songwriter Emilio Estefan Jr., who had written the show's theme song that Shakira had sung. Even though she was no longer on the show, she had remained in touch with Estefan and

Ricky Martin—"Livin' la Vida Loca"

Puerto Rico's Ricky Martin was one of the first Latin American pop singers to achieve crossover success with English-speaking audiences. His first group, Mexico's boy band Menudo, achieved major success with Latin American audiences. In the early 1990s, Martin struck out on his own as a solo artist with the album *Ricky Martin*. His debut sold over five hundred thousand copies internationally, with most of his fan base in Latin America.

In 1999 Martin released his first English-language album, also titled *Ricky Martin*. While most of the record received regular radio play around the world, his biggest hit off the album was "Livin' la Vida Loca." The song was a colossal hit, climbing to number one on the pop and Latin charts in many different countries and continents around the world, including the United States, the United Kingdom, Argentina, Australia, Brazil, France, Greece, India, Israel, Italy, Japan, Guatemala, Mexico, Russia, and South Africa. The album became one of the top albums of 1999 in the United States, staying at the number one spot on the *Billboard* Top 200 Albums chart for weeks, and was certified platinum seven times. It sold over 17 million copies worldwide, making Martin a Latin pop phenomenon around the world.

The numerous successes of Ricky Martin have made him a star all over the world.

his wife, Gloria, and now she wanted to hire him as her producer and manager.

Emilio instantly saw in Shakira a unique style and potential to be a crossover superstar—as big with worldwide mainstream audiences as she was with Latin American audiences. He and his wife took the young Shakira under their collective wing and began working on making the young Colombian an international star.

Chapter 3

A Star Is Born

Again, Shakira had linked herself with her perfect production partner—as executive producer, Estefan knew his main purpose for being in the studio was to make sure that audiences were hearing Shakira's music exactly as Shakira wanted them to hear it. While she had learned a lot about sound mixing and recording technology from Ochoa, she was still unsteady behind the controls themselves. "Technology scares me," she admits. "We live surrounded by a battalion of sounds, engaged in ostentatious displays of new recording techniques. To me, the fundamental essence of a song lies in the melody and the lyrics."[10]

On his part, Emilio loved Shakira's enthusiasm for learning everything she could about the music she was writing and recording. It was definitely to his credit that he was allowing Shakira to take charge of so many of the duties many producers jealously guard. Together, the two wrote, recorded, and produced the new album, eventually titled *¿Dónde Están los Ladrones?* (Where Are the Thieves?).

Major Hurdles

The album did not come without some major hurdles to get over. First of all, the budget for recording this new album turned out to be almost one hundred times that of her *Pies Descalzos*, coming in at a whopping $3 million before the CD was even released. Sony absolutely would not have allowed Shakira such a huge recording budget if Estefan had not been on board the project—his track record with previous recording artists was impeccable, however, and Sony figured that if he said such a huge budget was necessary, then it was probably worth the financial risk.

While still in preproduction, a briefcase containing all of Shakira's new lyrics was stolen at an airport before the vocal tracks had been recorded. Undaunted, Shakira wrote a whole new set of lyrics to accompany her music, and she was even happier with the new lyrics than she had been with the original.

The last hurdle was Shakira's insistence in naming the album after the song of the same name, a blatant finger-pointing song about political corruption in Colombia and in the United States. Some Sony executives were worried that she might scare off conservative audiences by wearing her political opinions so openly on her sleeve. By now, though, Shakira was used to dealing with record company executives, and in the end, the album looked, sounded, and was titled exactly the way she wanted it to be.

Crossover Appeal

When it finally came out in 1998, *¿Dónde Están los Ladrones?* broke through both the U.S. and Hispanic markets, spending eleven weeks at number one on *Billboard's* Latin album chart and hitting two number one spots on the Latin singles chart with the songs "Ciega, Sordomuda" (Blind, Deaf-Mute) and "Tú" (You). The album's signature track was the worldwide hit "Ojos Así" (Eyes Like Those). For this song, Shakira drew heavily on the Arabic music she had listened to as a small child sitting beside her father's desk, watching him write. It even had a verse written and sung completely in Arabic—something Shakira had not attempted in her earlier work. It was also a song that lent itself well to the belly-dancing act that Shakira had brought with her from her childhood to the international concert stage.

The album went multiplatinum in the United States, Colombia, Argentina, Chile, Mexico, Central America, and Spain. It sold over 8 million copies internationally at its release and eventually won Shakira two Latin Grammy Awards. Shakira was fast becoming one of the best-selling Latin American performers of all time. There was little chance that people were going to forget Shakira anytime soon.

Mutual Admiration

Even though she was still relatively unknown outside of the Latin-speaking world, Shakira's name was beginning to pop up everywhere. Even world-renowned Colombian novelist and Nobel Prize winner Gabriel García Márquez took special note of Shakira, dedicating an entire four pages to Shakira in his men's magazine, *Hombre de Cambio*.

Shakira returned the compliment by claiming that Márquez's internationally best-selling novel, *One Hundred Years of Solitude*, was one of her favorite books because it allowed people around the world to get to know a piece of her country's idiosyncrasies.

Shakira and Márquez eventually met and became close friends. Many people in the media speculated that there was more to their friendship than either Shakira or the much-older Márquez would admit, but Shakira shrugged off all such comments with dignity and extreme disapproval.

Amphibious

After being cooped up in the studio for so long, Shakira was anxious to get out on the road to promote her new album. She decided to make this tour significantly shorter and less physically grueling than her last tour, keeping it to just over three months long and confined to South America. The *Tour Anfibo,* or Amphibious Tour, started in March 2000 in Panama City and ended in Buenos Aires in mid-May. Shakira chose the name of her tour because she felt amphibious about herself at that point in her life: earthy, connected to the elements, adaptable, and willing to change when necessary. The stage show consisted of songs from both *Pies Descalzos* and *¿Dónde Están los Ladrones?* In addition, she included an a capella song, "Alfonsina y el Mar (Alfonsina and the Sea)," in her set, which had originally been written and performed by Argentinian folk singer Mercedes Sosa. Despite claims from critics that Shakira had lip-synched her way through some of the performances, nearly every concert along the tour route was almost instantly sold out.

Gabriel García Márquez: Poet and Philosopher

Gabriel García Márquez was born in 1928 in the small town of Aracataca, situated in a tropical region of northern Colombia, between the mountains and the Caribbean Sea. He grew up with his maternal grandfather, who was a pensioned colonel from the civil war at the beginning of the century.

Márquez went to a Jesuit college and began to read law, but his studies were soon broken off for his work as a journalist. In 1954 he was sent to Rome on an assignment for his newspaper and never came back, considering himself in self-exile from his country. He has lived all over the world, including Paris, New York, Spain, and Mexico, and has produced an enormous amount of nonfiction and fiction in Spanish, working closely with others to translate his work into almost every other language in the world. Unlike Shakira, Márquez was content to continue writing in Spanish and letting others rewrite his work in English, even after becoming fluent in English himself. His best-known books include the Nobel Prize–winning *One Hundred Years of Solitude* (*Cien Años de Soledad,* published in 1967), *In Evil Hour (La Mala Hora*, published in 1962), and his amazing debut collection of short stories, *Leaf Storm* (*La Hojarasca,* published in 1955).

Gabriel García Márquez and Shakira became close friends.

Shakira and her fiancé Antonio de la Ruá attended the
2001 Grammy Awards together. They met during
Shakira's Amphibious Tour.

During the tour, she met the man who would eventually become her fiancé, Antonio de la Ruá. Their eyes met across the room while eating at a crowded restaurant in Buenos Aires, and apparently something magical passed between the two. Later that day, de la Ruá appeared at the door of Shakira's dressing room and asked her out for a date. "I didn't know who he was, I just knew it was love at first sight,"[11] says Shakira. Shakira had caught the eye of South America's most eligible bachelor, a dashing lawyer whose father, Fernando de la Ruá, was the president of Argentina.

Soon after that first meeting, the two were officially a couple, and they went public to the press about their relationship. Shakira moved to Argentina to be near de la Ruá. However, their timing could not have been worse. News of their romance broke just as thirty thousand antigovernment protesters took to the streets of Buenos Aires. Commentators condemned the couple's lavish lifestyle, suggesting they pay off the national debt instead of parading their wealth around and living in a house rumored to be worth millions of dollars. Perhaps in retaliation against critics who claimed she was living too extravagant a lifestyle, Shakira decided it was time to start using her position of wealth and influence to help those less fortunate than herself. She started the foundation Pies Descalzos specifically to provide education materials, food, and clothing to poor children in South America, concentrating the focus especially on her home country of Colombia.

Crossover Success

The last trek of the *Tour Anfibo* took Shakira to the United States, where she had been invited to perform on the television show

MTV Unplugged. It was to be the channel's first Spanish-language broadcast ever. Performing in the Grand Ballroom of MTV's beautifully ornate Manhattan Center Studios in New York City, the Colombian singer sang almost all of the songs for which she had become well known for a live audience, including some new material she had begun working on during her tour.

MTV's editors took all of the taped footage and distilled it into an hour-long program that focused largely on the most important and influential songs of her repertoire. In 2000 the program was aired throughout Latin America, and later, after it was obvious that the show would perform as well in the ratings in North America, it aired in the United States. An album of the event, *MTV Unplugged,* was released in early 2000 and topped the Latin charts for two weeks on its way to becoming Shakira's third straight platinum album.

Tim Mitchell, who coproduced the *MTV Unplugged* album, was amazed at the young star's boundless self-confidence and her ability to connect intimately with all of her fans, even when there were thousands of them.

A New Manager

The record made from the *MTV Unplugged* session won Shakira a Grammy for best Latin pop album—her first of many such awards. Shakira was invited to perform at the very first Latin Grammy Awards ceremony in 2000. At the show, Shakira brought her music and her belly-dancing act both to the ceremony attendees and to millions of television viewers around the world, performing "Ojos Así." She took home trophies for best female pop vocal ("Ojos Así") and best female rock vocal ("Octavo Día" [The Eighth Day]).

One person who saw Shakira's early U.S. television performances was legendary manager Freddy DeMann, who had helped Michael Jackson's solo career, introduced the world to Madonna, and signed Alanis Morissette to her first major record deal. DeMann was watching a Latin music awards show on television when he spotted Shakira singing with Melissa Etheridge.

Shakira looks at her three platinum albums.

DeMann immediately got in touch with Shakira, and in 2000 replaced Emilio Estefan as her manager. The parting between Shakira and Emilio was a gracious one, and Shakira continued to look to both Estefans for studio help and advice.

Shakira performs with Emilio Estefan Jr., Jon Secada, and Jose Feliciano at the finale of the first Latin Academy of Recording Arts and Sciences Person of the Year award dinner tribute and concert in 2000.

A New Language

As soon as Shakira was settled back at home, Gloria Estefan suggested that she try rereleasing a few of the hits off *¿Dónde Están los Ladrones?* in English—in particular, the international hit "Ojos Así." When Shakira showed reluctance at trying to rewrite the song in English—a language she did not speak—Gloria offered to do the translation herself for Shakira to sing.

While she did let Gloria translate "Ojos Así" into the English "Eyes Like Yours," Shakira had already decided that the next step in her career was for her to master the English language herself. Relying on others for lyrics made her feel handicapped and dependent. "I

Gloria Estefan: Strength and Courage

Gloria Estefan's first public musical performance was at a large Cuban wedding when her future husband, Emilio Estefan Jr., asked her to join Miami Sound Machine onstage. A few weeks later, she became the lead singer for the band. The Miami Sound Machine released its first LP in 1977, making it the first all-Spanish album from CBS International.

In 1988 Gloria took top billing as the band's name changed to Gloria Estefan and the Miami Sound Machine, and in 1989 the group's name was dropped altogether and Estefan was credited as a solo artist. In 1989 she released her best-selling album to date, *Cuts Both Ways,* the title of which refered to Estefan's desire to appeal to both English- and Spanish-speaking fans. The album sold more than 10 million copies worldwide and reached number one in several countries.

While touring in support of *Cuts Both Ways,* a tractor trailer crashed into Gloria's tour bus in Pennsylvania, critically injuring her and breaking her back. She was flown by helicopter to New York City, where surgeons permanently implanted two titanium rods to stabilize her spinal column. Her grueling recovery took almost a year, and doctors told her she might not be able to walk again.

After extensive physical therapy, Gloria returned to the charts in 1991 with the album *Into the Light.* The *Into the Light World Tour* covered one hundred cities in nine countries and was seen by more than 10 million people worldwide. She continues to tour and perform to this day.

Gloria Estefan's career has spanned decades.

can't hire other people to write songs for me," she explained. "I have to write them myself."[12]

Taking Her Time

The release of the *Unplugged* album bought Shakira enough time to prepare for her next album. For the next two years, Shakira dedicated herself to learning English. With the help of a private tutor, she began to read English literature and song lyrics in earnest, trying to figure out how to make English work for her music. In particular, she read the poetry of Walt Whitman and the lyrics of everyone from Leonard Cohen to Bob Dylan.

The Estefans and DeMann were excited that Shakira was making the plunge into becoming a crossover star, and Gloria in particular was extremely supportive of her efforts. As an international star herself, she understood the doors that would open for Shakira if she could write music for mainstream English-speaking audiences. While many artists can achieve various levels of success staying in Latin America, most who become huge successes do so by becoming huge in the United States. Gloria herself got her break in the mid 1980s working with the Miami Sound Machine, while others, such as Selena and Ricky Martin, began their careers in Latin America and were discovered there, then brought to the United States, where they become tremendously successful.

"In the beginning, it was very intimidating. I wasn't sure if I was able to really write that good, and I was full of insecurities," says Shakira about learning English. "But there was like a little voice inside me, telling me strongly that was the step I had to take. I had to embrace new challenges in my life. And really, learning English wasn't that hard. It was just different."[13]

Chapter 4

Living in America

For Shakira, convincing herself that she could write even one good song, much less a whole album, entirely in a language foreign to her was a big challenge. "The first song I wrote by myself for this record was 'Objection,'" she remembers. "I prayed and asked God to send me a good song, and I remember I started writing the song a couple of hours after. I wrote the music and lyrics at the same time. When that happens, it's really magical to me,"[14] she added.

Once she had written "Objection," she knew that she could write more. Thinking a radical change of scenery was a necessary backdrop to composing such a radically different album, she packed up her poetry books, an English-language rhyming dictionary, her family, and her crew—which included producers Lester Mendez, Luis Fernando Ochoa, and executive producer Rick Rubin—and headed off to the countryside of Uruguay.

Even though he was not brought along for the trip, Emilio Estefan was more than happy to hype his young protégée to the press, hinting at what sort of record they could expect to hear from Shakira when she emerged from seclusion. He even told *Entertainment Weekly* that he fully expected Shakira to be the next big Latin crossover star, creating a sensation on the same scale as Selena or Ricky Martin. He predicted that Middle Eastern music combined with Latin music would be the next big sound. The isolated location made it easy for Shakira to dedicate all of her time to writing and recording without distraction. There, in a beautiful and isolated estate farm in Punta del Este, her crew set up a small recording studio, and Shakira began working on her first entirely English-language album.

Her time in Uruguay was relatively uneventful and very productive, up until the last weeks of recording. As she was adding the finishing touches to the new album, the mansion where she, her mother, and Antonio de la Ruá were staying was broken into and robbed. Very little of value was taken, suggesting that the thieves knew who was staying at the house and had been search-

Shakira poses with her platinum record, **Laundry Service.**

ing for things of sentimental value to Shakira and her fans and not things of real financial worth. Shaken by the break-in, Shakira's party left abruptly for Colombia.

9/11

By early September 2001, Shakira was in the United States, getting ready for the blitz of interviews that were guaranteed to accompany the announcement of a new record. While the new album, titled *Laundry Service*, was not available to the general public yet, many music reviewers for magazines, newspapers, and radio stations had been sent prerelease copies of the album. This is done so that prior to an album's release, music critics can share their opinions of an album with their readers so that when the album does come out, their readers have a general idea of whether they will like that album or not.

Soon after her arrival in Los Angeles, Shakira, along with the rest of the world, received news of the U.S. World Trade Center bombing on September 11, 2001. Shakira immediately spoke out against the terrorist attacks, determined to let people know that "the Arabic world is not all Muslims, nor are all Muslims terrorists." She added, "My father is 100 percent Lebanese, and he is not a terrorist. I come from a Catholic Arabic family, and I have never even met a terrorist in my whole life." She worried that the United States would go to war because of the tragedy, and that "the entire world might suffer for the irresponsible acts committed by a few people." [15]

When critics suggested that Shakira's opinions on the matter were not important, and that "pop stars should leave their political statements in their hotel rooms," she vehemently disagreed. "I am a pop star, but I also have an opinion," she said. "I grew up in a country that has existed under the whip of violence for 40 years, so how can I not? You know, in my country, a 5-year-old kid knows not only of Disney and Mickey Mouse, but also of guerrillas and paramilitaries. You grow up with that kind of awareness, of what the world is really like." [16]

Like a Volcano

With this new record, Shakira was determined to make what she considered her first truly rock album, something that drew directly from the music that had so heavily influenced her teen years. She enlisted the help of engineer Terry Manning, who had worked with 1970s groups like AC/DC and Led Zeppelin and contemporary performer Lenny Kravitz.

By October 2001 Shakira's fourth album, *Laundry Service*, was ready to be unleashed. Instead of releasing the entire album at once, Shakira decided to allow only one song off the album, "Whenever, Wherever," to be released as a teaser in advance of the album. A video of the song was also recorded and sent to MTV at the same time.

By now the Sony executives had learned their lesson and were 100 percent behind Shakira and her ideas, and they were willing to go the extra mile to promote her new album. "She's like a volcano waiting to explode into the Anglo market," Sony Music chairman Thomas D. Mottola said. "I will do whatever it takes to break her here, no matter how long it takes. We're in it for the long haul with Shakira." [17]

Shakira insisted on coming up with her own concept for the video and even brought a scribbled list of conditions when she first met video director Francis Lawrence. She wanted people watching the video to feel like they were making a journey. The scenes should be natural and outdoors, not confined and cybernetic. The star should stick to one outfit, because she wanted the video to be about the music, not what she was wearing. Lawrence apparently had come to the meeting with his own set of scribbled notes, and the two hashed it out for some time before settling on what the video should be.

After much negotiation, Lawrence and Shakira settled on shooting the video on a Universal Studios soundstage in front of a fake, snowcapped volcano, instead of the more natural setting that Shakira had originally planned on using. Shakira's other compromise was that there would be no footage shown of the backup musicians playing the native Andean instruments heard briefly on the pop-rock tune dominated by electric guitars. Shakira had especially wanted viewers to see the *quena* (pan flute) and *charango* (small guitar) being played, since she had specifically wanted to have those instruments played live on the album, instead of just using synthesizer

Shakira entered the mainstream pop market very quickly.

patches or MIDI samples. However, Lawrence could not find a way to integrate the live musicians with the scenes of Shakira bungee jumping off the volcano, so Shakira agreed they should let those scenes go.

Scaling the Charts

Both the video and the single climbed the charts rapidly, and it was obvious that Shakira was going to have no problem being accepted by English-speaking audiences. At the time of its release, "Whenever, Wherever" was the fourth fastest-rising song in its second week on the *Billboard* Radio & Records pop chart, while the video was the third most-played on MTV.

"For her foray into the mainstream pop market, she's off to a roaring start," [18] said Kevin McCabe, the publication's director of charts, soon after the record's release. Thanks to the early release of the "Whenever, Wherever" single and music video, Shakira had an English-speaking audience waiting for her new album even before it was available in stores. When *Laundry Service* was finally released in November 2001, it became one of the top twenty best sellers in the United States, debuting at number three on the *Billboard* charts.

The Language Barrier

Even though many critics and listeners were amused at Shakira's sometimes clumsy approach to putting English phrases together, nearly everyone agreed that the same clumsy phrases were highly imaginative and unique. For example, on "Whenever, Wherever," Shakira promised to "climb the Andes solely to count the freckles on your body," which sounded funny to some critics. However, the song was originally written by Shakira in Spanish with a different title, "Suerte," and in the Spanish version, she was counting *lunares*, which means moles or beauty spots and evokes the romanticism of the moon, or *luna*. On the song "Ready for the Good Times," Shakira reminisced about close encounters with roaches and living in squalor, while on "The One," she sang about rewarding her true love by shaving her legs and learning how to cook.

The most talked-about line in any of her songs, however, came from the single "Whenever, Wherever," where Shakira sings, "Lucky that my breasts are small and humble/So you don't confuse them with mountains."[19] Apparently, Shakira had been contemplating surgical breast enhancement at the time of the album's making, but changed her mind.

"I wrote that line because I've learnt to accept myself," says Shakira. "There've been moments when I've considered cosmetic surgery. But you start with lips, then breasts, then wrinkles and then you can't recognize yourself in the mirror anymore. It's like an addiction."[20]

The Hair Controversy

On the video and on the cover of her new album, Shakira surprised longtime fans by having bleach-blond hair instead of her natural, nearly black tresses—a move many disappointed Latin American fans criticized as being done specifically to cater to white U.S. audiences. Certain quarters interpreted this as a betrayal, quite literally, of her roots.

"I decided to become a blonde because I wanted a change," said Shakira in response to the hair controversy. "I'm human, after all. When I saw myself in the mirror I wanted to see something different." She added, "I loved being a redhead when I was younger, but it was not practical. I lived near the ocean, and every time I would go to the beach it would fade so quickly. I swear the water I was swimming in would become pink. It was embarrassing."[21]

While many longtime Shakira fans claimed that the new English-language record was just another sign that Shakira was trying to shed her Latin roots, there were some American critics already familiar with Shakira's work that complained that the English-language songs were lyrically much tamer and more clean-cut than her Spanish-language releases had been. Much of her

Shakira was criticized by fans for changing her hair color to blond.

previous work had been less about being in love and more about being angry and independent than the songs on *Laundry Service*.

Shakira claimed that her relationship with Antonio de la Ruá was partly responsible for the overall positive feel of the new album. "I think I am celebrating life more than ever," she said. "I had a slightly narrow vision of love. Now I am feeling unguarded, and it feels great. I feel washed clean of the way I looked at things in the past, which is why I am calling the album 'Laundry Service.'"[22]

A New Home

In early 2002 Shakira and Antonio de la Ruá moved from Argentina to a house in Miami, Florida, partly because it was more convenient for Shakira to work with her mostly U.S.-based staff, and partly because life was becoming increasingly difficult for the de la Ruá family in Argentina. Antonio's father, then President Fernando de la Ruá, found himself at the helm of a sinking country. Argentina was facing complete economic collapse, and de la Ruá was the perfect scapegoat. In 2002 de la Ruá resigned from office and a new administration took over. Fernando de la Ruá and his wife, Inés Pertiné, fled the country in disgrace.

The new administration tried to remove any traces of the old government, and one of their early targets was Shakira. All of the pop star's albums were taken off the shelves at the Tower Records stores in Argentina under the assumption that she would create support for the old regime due to her association with Antonio de la Ruá. It did not help Shakira's case that de la Ruá had appeared briefly in the music video for her big hit, "Underneath Your Clothes." *Laundry Service* itself had already sold more than seventy-five thousand copies in Argentina at the time of the ban, and the removal of such a popular performer's albums resounded as a bad move for

the record store chain, garnering criticism all the way to Tower Records' corporate headquarters.

"It's surprising to us that Tower Records Argentina would wage a negative campaign against such a respected artist,"[23] said Luana Pagani, Sony senior vice president of marketing for Latin America. The ban was lifted three days later, and Shakira's albums were flying off the shelves once again.

Another reason the couple left Argentina was that Shakira and de la Rúa's lives were under constant scrutiny by the press. Photographers followed the couple around everywhere they went, and newspapers and magazines speculated wildly about their relationship. Many Latin American pop stars have relocated to the United States simply because of U.S. laws that protect an individual's privacy, even if they are a public figure.

"I've always had a good relationship with journalists," explains Shakira. "I answer what I feel I should—and what I don't feel I should, I don't. But with the paparazzi, it was really crazy. I had never seen anything like that: 50-year-old guys climbing trees like monkeys to be able to take pictures of me and my boyfriend—to catch us holding hands! I mean, it's pretty obvious that if somebody is dating somebody they're gonna hold hands at some point, right?"[24]

Despite all of her attempts to maintain her privacy, Shakira's romance with Antonio de la Rúa had been a popular front-page topic in Argentina. When the de la Rúa family was embroiled in scandal, many of Shakira's inner circle advised her to separate from Antonio to distance herself from the scandal and protect her image. The move to Miami was, in many ways, the easiest way for Shakira to end the media problems plaguing her personal life.

Soon, she and Antonio de la Rúa had purchased a mansion with room for a recording studio in it rumored to be worth several million dollars on Old Fort Bay in Miami, Florida. The mansion was complete with a guardhouse for protection from prying eyes, as well as another house for her parents and her brother,

Argentina's Troubled Presidency

Fernando de la Rúa Bruno was president of Argentina for almost exactly two years, from December 1999 to December 2001. He was the leader of the Alianza political party, which was an alliance between the Radical Civic Union and the Frepaso party.

De la Rúa was one of the youngest politicians in Argentina's recent history, elected as a senator in Buenos Aires by the time he was thirty-five and running for the position of Ricardo Balbín's vice president by the time he was thirty-six. Because he was so young, he was given the nickname "Chupete" (Pacifier), a nickname that stuck with him throughout his time in government office.

He became president of Argentina in 1999, winning the election with almost 50 percent of the votes. Unfortunately, his presidency was cursed right from the start. He was now head of a country plagued by an ongoing economic crisis and a government full of corruption. He was finally forced out of office after several weeks of violent demonstrations and street riots.

Shakira talks with Argentina's president Nestor Kirchner and his wife, Cristina Fernandez, before her 2006 concert in Argentina.

Alanis Morissette: Canada's Own Rock Prodigy

When Shakira's third album, the rock-edged *Pies Descalzos*, came out, people were quick to compare her to Canadian songstress Alanis Morissette, another young female performer who wrote songs with similar musical themes.

In reality, the two stars shared much more than just a love for girl-power rock music. Like Shakira, Alanis began writing music at an early age. Also like Shakira, Alanis began appearing on children's television shows by the time she was ten—Alanis was a cast member on the hit children's TV show *You Can't Do That on Television*. She also appeared briefly as a contestant on *Star Search*, but she lost after one round.

With the money she made from being on TV, Alanis recorded and released a single featuring two of her songs, "Fate Stay with Me" and "Find the Right Man." Even though the single went relatively unnoticed, Alanis was getting attention as a musical performer and was invited to perform with the Orpheus Musical Theatre Society.

In 1990 Alanis was signed to MCA Records Canada and released her debut album, *Alanis*. The album reached the Top Ten on the Canadian charts, and the twenty-three-year-old soon became one of the hottest female performers in the world. Over the next fifteen years, she released ten critically acclaimed full-length albums and dozens of spin-off singles.

Tonino, close by. Just as when she was on tour, Shakira and her parents would get together several times a week to eat dinner and talk. While many things in her life were changing, her relationship with her family was one thing she was determined would stay the same.

Chapter 5

What Is a Mongoose?

Even though they were not embroiled in the middle of a political scandal like they had been in Argentina, Shakira and Antonio de la Ruá were far from safe from the press. Almost from the day that they moved to the United States, the couple quickly became a subject of fascination for Miami-area gossip columns. The attention was mostly positive, however, and the only real jabs at her character had to do with speculation on how much Shakira's new house—a five-bedroom mansion with a swimming pool and a recording studio—had cost the Colombian songstress.

Almost immediately after the record *Laundry Service* hit the stores, Shakira was appearing on radio shows and in magazines around the world. She even appeared on the covers of *Time* and *Newsweek* magazines. The album sold 13 million copies by the end of 2001, with over 3 million sales in the United States alone. Everyone who owned a magazine or a television or radio station wanted to hear what Shakira had to say about her new record, her plans for the future, her relationship with de la Ruá, and everything in between.

Soon after moving to America, Shakira drew the attention of Pepsi executives who thought she would make the perfect spokesperson for their product. It was not long before gigantic billboards sporting Shakira's face smiling behind a bottle of Pepsi sprouted along highways from coast to coast, while her television commercials were considered by many to be the most popular Pepsi ad campaign since the company had hired Michael

Jackson to glamorize the product nearly twenty years before. According to the *National Enquirer*, the starlet began crying when she saw a playback of the first version of the Pepsi commercial. She apparently hated the way she looked in the video and demanded the production shut down for a day while a stylist wove in hair extensions.

A Familiar Face

Shakira was becoming almost as well known a television personality as she was a recording artist. Over the span of a year, she appeared on numerous late-night talk shows and variety entertainment shows, including *The Tonight Show with Jay Leno*, *Saturday Night Live*, and *Mad TV*, both as a guest and as a musical performer. In May 2002 she appeared on VH1's *Divas Las Vegas* special, which also featured performances by Cher and the Dixie Chicks. The following December, she was invited—along with David Bowie—to perform on Dick Clark's *Primetime Rockin' New Year's Eve* to fill a last-minute cancellation by the Who.

Her music and her belly dancing were not the only things causing a stir among her new American audience—the clothes she wore while on TV were receiving almost as much press as the star herself. Girls across the United States copied Shakira's ripped-jeans-and-vintage-T-shirt look, and her wild, curly, blonde tresses were appearing on the heads of girls aged twelve and up. For a short while, the puka shell bracelet Shakira wore on her *Mad TV* performance was a hot fashion accessory in the stores—until it was revealed that the bracelet had been a gift from a fan given to Shakira shortly before the performance, and not the long-cherished keepsake trend spotters had thought it to be. Toy manufacturer Mattel even announced they were planning to create a Shakira doll for her younger fans. Calvin Klein, jumping on the fact that Shakira already wore jeans on a near-daily basis, hired her as a model and spokesperson for their company.

The Price of Celebrity

As sales totals of Shakira's album swept toward a worldwide total of 25 million, she was beginning to realize how difficult it was to be a star. During an in-store appearance and autograph signing by Shakira in Melbourne, Australia, over two thousand fans were refused admission to the Virgin Megastore for not already owning a copy of *Laundry Service*.

One angry fan, a nineteen-year-old man, threw a bag of cement dust at the Colombian pop singer, and although Shakira herself was not hit, at least twenty fans suffered breathing difficulties when the bag broke open. One girl was treated for an asthma attack. Despite the distraction, Shakira continued to sign autographs for

Shakira signs autographs before her appearance on NBC's Today Show.

the five hundred fans who had been allowed inside for an hour and a half after the cement incident. After the in-store appearance, she met with the fans who needed to have medical attention because of the attack.

Although Shakira enjoyed all the attention her new album received, her one true love remained performing her music live in concert. Performing for television studio audiences is very different from performing for arena concert audiences. Not only is a television audience much smaller, but many times, there just is not room for a live band to accompany a singer in a television studio, and often the performer is expected just to lip-synch their way through their performance. After an exhausting round of tel-

A crowd gathers outside the Virgin Megastore in New York's Times Square for the signing of Shakira's new album, Fijación Oral, Vol. 1.

evision show performances, Shakira decided it was time to get out of the recording studio—and studio audiences—and back out on the road to connect with her audiences on a more personal level. So she started planning a new, worldwide tour.

"I must tell you, that it's the show of my dreams," the twenty-five-year-old Shakira told reporters during tour rehearsals in Miami. "It's definitely a rock show. I feel that I'm a rocker trapped in a pop-singer body, and finally the rocker is going to have its opportunity to come out."[25]

The *Tour of the Mongoose*

In 2003 Shakira began the first leg of her *Tour de la Mongosta* (*Tour of the Mongoose*), which was scheduled to visit fifty cities in thirty different countries. In preparation for the tour, Shakira made an unusual move. She hired a history tutor from New York University to come along and show her all the important historic sites along the U.S. leg of her tour. She was determined to learn as much as possible about her new home country, and bringing a U.S. history professor seemed the most logical way to do so.

She told reporters that she had chosen the name *Tour of the Mongoose* because the mongoose was the only animal that can survive a cobra bite, and that the title of the tour was a metaphor for the struggle of good against evil. "The cobra is deadly, but the mongoose can overcome it," she said. "We all have the possibility to defeat prejudice and resentment in our lives. Fear is the thing that makes us attack, that makes us strike, but we must overcome it. We must."[26]

Her Heart on Her Sleeve

While she had never been one to shy away from controversy, with this tour, Shakira now seemed determined to get everyone around her involved in politics. Her stage show featured gigantic screens depicting puppets of Saddam Hussein and George Bush playing chess, broken up by footage shot in real wars. By the end of the film, it was revealed that the puppeteer was the Grim Reaper. "Bite the neck of hatred," read the farewell line on the screens at the end of the show.

Shakira said about the show:

> I think that we see war as a virtual thing and we even get to believe that bombs fall on top of cardboard cutouts and stuff like that. They don't. They kill real people, real children, real mothers and millions of innocent people. I come from Colombia, which is a country that has been under the whip of violence for more than four decades, so I've seen the consequences of war and I've seen the psychological damage that it does in a society. And I think that we're never ready for war. [27]

Shakira went on to criticize pop star Madonna for censoring her own politics. Madonna's 2003 video for her song "American Life" had originally been a strong antiwar message, containing footage of Madonna dressed as a soldier and throwing a grenade into the lap of President George W. Bush. The usually brash pop star ended up dumping the video weeks before its release because of the Iraq war, claiming she had withdrawn the video out of sensitivity and respect to the armed forces involved in the Iraq conflict.

"I'd expect a little more backbone from Madonna," said Shakira. "Good pop music is always political in times of crisis." [28]

Around the World

Shakira's blunt and powerful statements might have caused some disappointed audience members to boycott her show, or even her records, but in the big picture of things, no one would

UNICEF: Putting Celebrity to Good Use

In 2003 Shakira joined a world-class roster of celebrities who have embraced UNICEF through the years, dating back more than fifty years to the first UNICEF Goodwill Ambassador, Danny Kaye. Over the years Goodwill Ambassadors have been high-profile figures picked from the worlds of literature, sports, music, art, and film, and have come from every continent on the planet. Past Goodwill Ambassadors have included actresses Audrey Hepburn and Mia Farrow, musician Harry Belafonte, and actor Roger Moore. Far from being just another pretty celebrity face for a campaign, a UNICEF Goodwill Ambassador is expected to see firsthand some of the most desperate and poor parts of the world to report on everything from epidemics to human rights abuses.

Shakira joins the ranks of about one hundred famous faces selected as UN ambassadors for their pet projects. Former Spice Girl Geri Halliwell speaks out on birth-control issues, actor Michael Douglas petitions for nuclear disarmament, and actress Angelina Jolie works on refugee relief.

Shakira, Nana Mouskouri, Kofi Annan, and Maria Emma Mejia attend a UNICEF Goodwill gala. Shakira was named a UNICEF Goodwill Ambassador in late 2003.

have noticed. In November 2003 twelve thousand fans turned out to see Shakira perform in Toronto, Canada, while in April 2004 Shakira broke all previous concert-attendance records at Portugal's Atlantic Pavilion. In March 2004 she performed for a crowd of sixteen thousand in France, and in Argentina, where her music had previously been banned, she performed in May 2004 for a packed crowd of over fifty thousand— which included her fiancé's mother, Argentina's ex-first lady, Inés Pertiné.

"Some wanted to exile me, but you can't exile people from their land and, in a way, I am a part of you," Shakira told the packed River Plate audience at the beginning of her show in Argentina. "You can't imagine how special being here is to me." [29]

Shakira had originally planned on performing in several countries in the Middle East during the tour, including her father's home country of Lebanon, but had to cancel the concerts due to the war in Iraq. It was already difficult getting her entire entourage and stage equipment through customs inspections in Europe and the United States, and traveling through the Middle East on a tight schedule would have been nearly impossible, not to mention extremely dangerous.

Some news organizations in the Middle East took Shakira's show cancellations as a personal affront, claiming that the half-Lebanese Shakira was anti-Semitic. Other false allegations about Shakira also spread on the Internet claiming that the singer donated money to the Lebanese Hizballah movement.

Charitable Works

In late 2003 Shakira was named a UNICEF (United Nations Children's Fund) Goodwill Ambassador, making the twenty-six-year-old the youngest Goodwill Ambassador in the organization's history. A Goodwill Ambassador's duties are to travel to developing countries to witness poverty and injustice firsthand and bring an account back to the UN to discuss how to improve the conditions observed.

Shakira decided right away to make her focus the children of these countries, just as her Pies Descalzos Foundation had already done in South America. In her new role, Shakira would serve as a global representative of UNICEF, using her popularity and her personal interest in children's issues to support UNICEF's mission to improve the welfare of every child worldwide. Shakira also planned to work with UNICEF in its global battle to get poverty-stricken children into school and give them a quality basic education.

"UNICEF has done tremendous work in my home nation of Colombia and I have seen first-hand the difference UNICEF makes," said Shakira, who was also the first Colombian to be appointed a global Goodwill Ambassador. "It's rewarding to know that I join such a great list of stars supporting UNICEF, and can personally contribute to improving the lives and futures of children."[30]

Carol Bellamy, executive director of UNICEF, said about Shakira's appointment:

Fifty years ago, UNICEF was the first global organization to utilize the power of celebrity to further global causes when it named beloved entertainer Danny Kaye its first Goodwill Ambassador. Shakira, like all our Goodwill Ambassadors, was chosen based on her compassion, her involvement in global issues, her deep commitment to helping children, and her appeal to young people around the world.[31]

One of her first trips as a UNICEF ambassador was to her home country of Colombia to visit some of the towns that had been struck hardest by depression. Her visit to the small town of Quibdó, in particular, seemed to strike a nerve in her. She was moved to tears while visiting some of the young beneficiaries of her Pies Descalzos Foundation and was apparently astonished at how much more work she would have to do to make a difference in such a poverty-stricken area.

Not long after, she partnered up with the Reebok Human Rights Program to start a year-long project to distribute ten thousand pairs of Reebok shoes to Colombia's neediest chil-

Quibdó: The Poorest of the Poor

When Shakira visited Quibdó, the capital city of the province of Chocó, Colombia, she was moved to tears by the poverty she found there. For most Colombians, Chocó is an unknown territory and is normally seen as a place to avoid rather than a place to visit. Bordering on the Pacific coast and Panama, it is a strategically important area for the illegal armed groups struggling to control the region. It is also probably the richest region in terms of biodiversity on the planet and is full of dramatically beautiful rain forests and wildlife, all of which are threatened by mining and lumber companies run by international corporations.

Quibdó has no more than 120,000 inhabitants, including approximately 25,000 homeless people from different rural areas of the province. In Quibdó, poverty lies on every corner. There is no industry, and most of the few jobs available are provided by the government. Poor hygiene and sanitation conditions, erratic energy supplies, limited health and education facilities, and insufficient waste management all contribute to create problems in this town.

dren, beginning in Shakira's hometown of Barranquilla. Her own foundation work expanded from building schools and providing educational supplies to supporting and funding hospitals and community programs aimed at benefiting the children of Colombia.

Her efforts in Colombia did not go unnoticed. In gratitude, a 16-foot (4.88m) steel statue of Shakira was erected in her hometown of Barranquilla. Designed and donated to the city by German sculptor Dieter Patt, the 5-ton (4.54-metric ton) statue is dressed in bell-bottomed pants and has a guitar strapped to its neck.

While some people were recognizing Shakira for her important charity work, still others were taking note of the pop star for more superficial reasons. In late 2003 Shakira was named Loveliest Latin Lady by *Stuff* magazine, beating out Jennifer Lopez, fellow Colombian Sofia Vergara, Mexico's Salma Hayek, and Cuba's Daisy Fuentes. A magazine insider admitted surprise at Shakira winning the poll, claiming that "no one expected Shakira to finish first." [32]

Chapter 6

Taking Chances and Making a Difference

Despite her extensive tour in 2003, Shakira realized that she had been off the radar for a long time. Four years between album releases amounts to an eternity in the world of popular music, especially when a star's primary audience is the youth market. Fans get older and forget the pop stars they liked when they were younger, so new audiences have to be cultivated continuously.

"How things are now in the music industry, you've got to be putting out a new record every six months—we are like hamburgers," she said. "I just can't do it that way." [33]

Once again, in order to allow herself some time to work on an album of new material, Shakira decided to release two new records of old material. The first, released in 2002 just before her tour, was a compilation titled *Grandes Éxitos* (Greatest Hits), which featured songs from all of her previously released albums—including the first two albums that had only been released to audiences in South America. The CD came with a DVD of Shakira's music videos, including the popular "Whenever, Wherever/Suerte."

The second album, released just months after she was back home from touring, was called *Live & Off the Record* (2004). *Live & Off the Record* was another CD/DVD collection that documented the *Tour of the Mongoose* in support of *Laundry Service*. Both discs included

Shakira's rendition of AC/DC's 1980 anthem "Back in Black," which had been met with mixed reactions from audiences but was a song apparently very close to Shakira's heart. On the DVD, Shakira allowed a camera crew unlimited access to shoot backstage footage of her tour. Shakira admitted the movie did not always show her in the most positive light. "When my fans watch this documentary, they are going to see that I'm a neurotic, that I'm an obsessive-compulsive perfectionist, and I don't know if they are going to like that, but they for sure will understand me a little more," [34] she said.

Back in the Studio

Confident that her audience would be satisfied with these two new releases, Shakira went to work in earnest on an album of brand-new material. The world tour had opened her eyes to exactly who her audience now was, and she wanted to make a record that would speak to all of them.

However, it was not long before she realized that there just was not enough space on one album to reach everyone she wanted to. So she decided that instead of writing one new album, she would write two at the same time—one in Spanish, one in English.

The fact that the Spanish-language album, *Fijación Oral, Vol. 1* (Oral Fixation, Vol. 1) came out first was not lost on her Latin American fans, who had felt that the Colombian-born Shakira was drawing away from her roots. The album entered the charts at number four on its June 15, 2005, release, making it the highest-ever debut for a Spanish-language album—breaking Ricky Martin's previous record for his 2003 release *Almas del Silencio. Fijación Oral* was much more than just a Spanish-language album, though—for this collection, Shakira also sang some verses in French and German, too, thinking those languages worked better with the music than either Spanish or English did.

Shakira and Alejandro Sanz perform at the 2006 Latin Grammy Awards.

"La Tortura"

Shakira drew even more attention to both herself and the record with the release of the music video for the song "La Tortura" (The Torture). The soap-opera-like video featured Shakira writhing around in mud with Spanish superstar Alejandro Sanz, with whom she had apparently spent part of the previous Christmas holiday. North American and South American tabloids alike suggested that the two of them were linked romantically, a suggestion Shakira scoffed at.

"Alejandro's voice was exactly what the song needed," was all she would say about their collaboration. "His voice is unique, raw, and absolutely sensual. He added a beautiful and unexpected vocal harmony. What can I say? I'm running his fan club now." [35]

The ensuing controversy may have been one of the reasons the video received so much attention, eventually becoming the only all-Spanish clip ever to be added to regular rotation on MTV. In fact, the April 26, 2005, episode of MTV's *Making the*

Alejandro Sanz

Alejandro Sanz, who performed with Shakira in her song "La Tortura," was already well known in his home country of Spain when Shakira helped introduce him to audiences in America. He self-released his first album when he was sixteen, but he had to wait until he was twenty-two for Warner Brothers to sign him on as a recording artist and release his official debut, *Viviendo Deprisa*, which sold over a million copies in Spain. Since then, his records have won multiple awards internationally, including the World Music Award for best-selling Spanish artist and fourteen Grammy Awards.

Video showed behind-the-scenes clips of "La Tortura" and ended with the premiere of the video. This was notably the first time the show had been aired entirely in Spanish (with English subtitles). The video also premiered on the show *Total Request Live* as the first Spanish-language music video ever to be included in its Top Ten countdown—it ranked number four in the countdown.

Later that year, Shakira nabbed two MTV Video Music Award nominations (best female video and best dance video). Two months after the album's release, she became the first singer to perform her set entirely in Spanish at the MTV Video Music Awards. She also appeared on ABC's *The View*, Univision's *Despierta América*, and *Good Morning America*. Immediately after the *Good Morning America* appearance, Shakira flew to Spain to sing three songs at Madrid's Puerta de Alcalá square as part of a huge free music festival.

She was also asked to perform at the Live 8 concert in Versailles, France, at King Louis XIV's Palace of Versailles, built in the seventeenth century and considered by many to be one of the most opulent homes of any ruler in history. Musicians from all over the world showed up at the concert to raise awareness of African poverty and pressure the world's most powerful leaders to recognize the continent's plight at the Group of Eight summit in Scotland taking place the following week. Nearly one hundred thousand people attended the international event.

A Two-Part Event

Fijación Oral, Vol. 1 was simultaneously released all over Latin America and charted at number one in almost all of its countries. In the United States it charted at number four on the *Billboard* Top 200 Albums chart and became the best-selling Spanish first-week-sales album (157,000), breaking Ricky Martin's self-titled album (charting at number twelve, selling 65,000). It was also well received in non-Spanish-speaking countries like Germany, where it reached number one, and Canada, where it reached number seven. *Fijación Oral, Vol. 1* was officially the most successful Latin music album of all time. More than 150,000 fans poured into Madrid's historic Puerta de Alcalá to see Shakira perform in celebration of the record's European release, and her New York appearance at the Virgin Megastore in Times Square drew masses of fans, closing down several city blocks. Thousands more showed up for subsequent autograph sessions in Miami and Puerto Rico.

In November 2005 the English-language album, *Oral Fixation, Vol. 2*, was released. The album featured fellow Latin American performer Carlos Santana playing guitar on one of the tracks. It also featured the professional church choir Seraphic Fire, making them the first choral music ensemble to be featured on a hit pop album since the Benedictine Monks of Silos sang on the 1990 Enigma album *MCMXC*. The Seraphic Fire ensemble was named after the angels (the seraph) that surround Yahweh's throne in heaven, angels whose singing is so loud that it shakes the very foundation of the palace.

Surprisingly, the English-language album did not sell as well as the Spanish-language one. It debuted at number 5 on the pop charts and dropped to number twenty-six only two weeks later. The album did slightly better in Europe, but still not as good as the Spanish-language album. It was turning out to be one of the greater ironies of Shakira's life that after working so hard to learn English to be a crossover artist, her highest-selling album was one written mostly in Spanish.

Learning to Compromise

Shakira's next move was to start promoting the two new albums, especially the second, as it seemed as though it was having a harder time breaking into the Top Ten charts. Some of her advisors believe that the cover artwork might have been one of the reasons customers were slower to pick up a copy of *Oral Fixation, Vol. 2*. The cover featured a photo of a topless Shakira partially hidden behind a tree and holding an apple—inspired by Albrecht

Shakira listens to a member of the press at the Virgin Megastore in New York. Her appearance drew masses of fans.

Durer's engraving of Adam and Eve—with a small child reaching for the apple in her hand. *Fijación Oral, Vol. 1*'s cover showed Shakira wearing a peasant dress and holding a baby in her lap, and it was significantly less controversial. The lyrical content of the two albums was signficantly different, too, with the Spanish-language album being more concerned with love and relation-ships and the English-language one being more political and socially oriented.

It was not long before *Oral Fixation, Vol. 2* was being pulled off record store shelves in the Middle East, while in Egypt, the cover was altered to avoid further upset. Furthermore, some countries with strong Muslim populations were banning the song "How Do You Do" from airplay because in the lyrics, Shakira

Shakira dances during the filming of her and Wyclef Jean's "Hips Don't Lie" music video.

questioned God. The song was eventually taken out of copies released to those countries, and the the cover was altered to show Shakira standing behind a bush, covered from her shoulders down.

One can only imagine what Shakira must have thought of all of these changes being made to her album. For someone who had insisted on having control of nearly every step of her career, down to doing her own translations, studio production work, and even her own stage makeup, having to make these compromises must have been difficult.

Everywhere at Once

The year 2006 was turning out to be a busy one for Shakira. In January, she performed at the NRJ Music Awards in Cannes, France, and received the Best International Song Award for the song "La Tortura." On February 8, 2006, Shakira received another Grammy Award, this time for *Fijación Oral, Vol. 1*. Even though *Oral Fixation, Vol. 2* did not win any awards, Shakira was determined that her English-language album, which had only sold about half as many copies as *Fijación Oral, Vol. 1*, was going to get the attention she thought it deserved.

The key to the album's eventual success lay in a unique partnership with music and hip-hop performer Wyclef Jean. Jean had an idea for a song he wanted to write for Shakira, and he had his manager call Shakira's manager, Freddy DeMann. DeMann called Shakira's house and left a message with a houseguest as Shakira was sleeping. According to Shakira, she had just had a dream about performing with Jean when her friend told her about the phone call. She immediately booked a flight to Miami to meet with Jean, and the two of them immediately went to work in the studio.

Their first song together was "Hips Don't Lie." The title came from Shakira's in-studio mantra about how her band members need to watch her hips to determine where a song they are working on needs to go. The story went that if she told them if the music made her hips move, then the song was working: hips don't lie. Shakira then took her private joke with the band and put it in the context of the song.

Shakira holds the four Latin Grammy Awards that she won in 2006.

A New Fixation

Shakira and Wyclef Jean were asked to perform at the Latin Billboard Music Awards, where they unveiled the new song. It was an instant hit. That night, Shakira also received five Latin Billboard Music Awards: one for *Fijación Oral, Vol. 1* and four awards for the song "La Tortura."

To her surprise, Shakira was also awarded a Spirit of Hope Award in recognition of her humanitarian work. Four children from her Pies Descalzos Foundation came onstage to present her with the award, and Shakira was visibly moved to tears.

Shakira knew that "Hips Don't Lie" was the song she needed to make *Oral Fixation, Vol. 2* the success she wanted it to be. She and Jean headed back into the studio to record the song, and a new version of *Oral Fixation, Vol. 2* was in the works, with "Hips Don't Lie" included as a bonus track, as well as an alternate Spanglish version of the *Fijación Oral, Vol. 1* hit "La Tortura."

Her hunch paid off. The new *Oral Fixation* skyrocketed into the Top Ten on the charts, ending its first week on the charts in the number six spot. It quickly went platinum, selling over a million copies in the United States. Both of Shakira's albums had debuted in the top five of the *Billboard* Top 200 Albums chart, making Shakira the only artist ever to debut top five albums in English and Spanish in the same calendar year. The album also went gold in nine other countries, including Canada, Mexico, Austria, Italy, Portugal, Spain, Argentina, Colombia, and India.

"Hips Don't Lie" fast became the biggest hit of 2006, and Shakira and Wyclef could be seen performing the song all over daytime TV, including *Live with Regis and Kelly*, *The Ellen DeGeneres Show*, and *The CBS Early Show*.

American Idol

In March 2006 Shakira and Jean were invited to appear on FOX TV's popular show *American Idol*. Shakira was excited about the invitation, until she found out she was not going to be allowed to bring her band on the show with her due to the show's financial constraints. Shakira threatened to cancel her performance, and the producers relented.

Even though her performance went off without a hitch, there was apparently still some bad blood between her and the station. After the performance, Shakira was apparently supposed to meet with the show's contestants, but instead, she left the studio almost immediately after the performance.

"She asked to meet with the contestants," said *American Idol* executive producer Nigel Lythgoe. "The only thing Shakira taught them last week was how to have a big entourage and be discourteous."[36]

Hearing about the fuss, Shakira wrote a letter of apology to the producers of the show, claiming she did not know the contestants were waiting for her and had snubbed them by accident.

Crusader for Kids

Shakira's political crusades were getting almost as much attention as her musical escapades. Along with other celebrity ambassadors, Shakira recorded a public service announcement for Unite for Children Unite Against AIDS, urging viewers to educate themselves on the danger of HIV/AIDS. "Millions of children are missing an education," Shakira says in the thirty-second television spot. "Missing their teachers who have died from the disease. Missing from class as they stay home to care for their dying mothers and fathers."[37]

Appointed by UNICEF in 2003, Shakira's main commitment as a Goodwill Ambassador has been education. "I'm a firm believer," she asserted, "that education is the most efficient tool we have to make people aware and make our children aware, and to protect them from the scourge of the century, which is AIDS."[38]

Shakira and Wyclef Jean perform during the 2006 MTV Video Music Awards.

Guns into Guitars

Audiences of Shakira's *Oral Fixation Tour* could not help but notice the guitar that Shakira brought with her on tour. The body of the guitar was built around parts of an AK-47 machine gun, with six metal guitar strings stretching from the midpoint of its wooden stock, across the loading chamber, past the fret board threaded over the weapon's barrel, and ending at the guitar neck flaring past the muzzle.

The guitar was designed by Colombian artist Cesar Lopez, a classically trained musician and composer who began designing instruments made out of decommissioned military weapons. The Colombian government officials who handed the machine guns over to Lopez had the firing pins removed so they could no longer be used as weapons.

Lopez is part of a group called the Battalion of Immediate Artistic Reaction. The group is made up of musicians and political activists who are tired of Colombia's four-decade-old war. Whenever they receive news of a guerrilla attack in Bogotá, Colombia, they take to the streets, playing music with their own "weapons" and serenading the victims with soothing music.

Shakira's guitar was given to her as a gift by Lopez, who also planned to give the guitars to other high-profile musicians such as Carlos Santana, Paul McCartney, and Carlos Vivas, as well as some political and religious leaders like the Dali Lama.

Colombian singer Cesar Lopez holds a shotgun transformed into a guitar. Lopez gave one to Shakira as a gift.

On April 3, 2006, the UN honored Shakira for her work with children in Colombia at their convention on Poverty, Women and Human Rights. The event was part awards ceremony, part fashion show, featuring clothes partly made by women trying to escape poverty in developing countries and sponsored by the nonprofit organization Women Together.

"Let's not forget at the end of this day when we all go home, 960 children will have died in Latin America," the five-time Grammy Award winner said after accepting her award. "That's the truth we cannot allow today—not today, not in this century, not belonging to this generation, the first generation that can actually provoke tangible changes in the world. Let's take advantage of this historical opportunity we have within reach to make this world a better place."[39]

Chapter 1: An Early Start

1. Quoted in VH1 show, "Shakira: Woman Child in the Promised Land," aired February 13, 2002.
2. Quoted in Mim Udovitch, "Underneath Shakira," *Rolling Stone*, February 2002. www.rollingstone.com/news/story/5931811/underneath_shakira
3. Quoted in Ximena Diego, *Shakira: Woman Full of Grace*. New York: Simon & Schuster, 2001.

Chapter 2: Finding Her Voice

4. Quoted in *Independent Online*, "Shakira: Rhythm Queen," January 28, 2006. http://enjoyment.independent.co.uk/music/features/article341367.ece.
5. Quoted in Adrian Deevoy, "Columbian Gold," *Blender*, April/May 2002.
6. Quoted in Mark Bautz, "Platinum Blond," *Entertainment Weekly*, December 18, 2001.
7. Gary Graff, "The Poet and the Princess," the *Guardian*, June 8, 2002. www.guardian.co.uk/colombia/story/0,11502,729652,00.html.
8. Quoted in Lauren Gitlin, "Shakira Breaking Barriers," *Rolling Stone*, November 2005.
9. Quoted in VH1 show, "Shakira: Woman Child in the Promised Land," aired February 13, 2002.

Chapter 3: A Star Is Born

10. Quoted in Ernesto Lechner, "Laundry Service," *Rolling Stone*, November 2001. www.rollingstone.com/reviews/album/314397/laundry_service.

11. Quoted in "Belly Dancing Diva with the Flaming Headdress," *Telegraph*, November 4, 2001. www.telegraph.co.uk/arts/main.jhtml?xml=/arts/2002/12/18/bmshak18.xml.
12. Quoted in Christopher John Farley, "The Making of a Rocker," *Time*, September 15, 2001. www.time.com/time/magazine/article/0,9171,1000767,00.html.
13. Quoted in Eleanor Black, "Nice Meeting the Little Big Star," *New Zealand Herald*, July 5, 2002.

Chapter 4: Living in America

14. Quoted in *Independent Online*, "Shakira."
15. Quoted in Bautz, "Platinum Blond."
16. Quoted in Nick Duerden, "The Sexiest Woman in Music Today: Shakira," *Blender*, March 2003. www.blender.com/guide/articles.aspx?id=121.
17. Quoted in Duerden, "The Sexiest Woman in Music Today: Shakira."
18. *Independent Online*, http://enjoyment.independent.co.uk. January 28, 2006. "Shakira: Rhythm Queen."
19. Quoted in *Independent Online*, "Shakira."
20. Quoted in Celebrityspider.com, July 30, 2005, "Shakira Keeps Her Small and Humble Breasts," www.celebrityspider.com/news/july05/article072905-20.html, from Shakira press release.
21. Quoted in Bautz, "Platinum Blond."
22. Quoted in Jordan Levin, "Shakira Offers New Take on Life and Love," *Miami Herald*, June 7, 2005.
23. Quoted in Evan Wright, "Latin America's Biggest Star Is Ready for You to Fall in Love with Her. Resistance Is Futile," *Rolling Stone*, April 15, 2002. www.rollingstone.com/artists/shakira/articles/story/5937750/shakira.
24. Quoted in Udovitch, "Underneath Shakira."

Chapter 5: What Is a Mongoose?

25. Quoted in Graff, "The Poet and the Princess."
26. Quoted in Duerden, "The Sexiest Woman in Music Today."
27. Quoted in Duerden, "The Sexiest Woman in Music Today."
28. Quoted in Ananova.com, April 25, 2003, Ananova, from Shakira press release, www.ananova.com/entertainment/story/sm_773998.html.
29. Quoted in Marcelo García Avila, "That's Why the Lady Is a Star," *Buenos Aires Herald*, February 8, 2006.
30. UNICEF Press Centre, "Singer and Songwriter Shakira Appointed UNICEF Goodwill Ambassador," www.unicef.org/media/media_15183.html.
31. Quoted in UNICEF.org, www.unicef.org/media/media_15183.html.
32. Quoted in Contactmusic.com, August 19, 2003, from Shakira press release. www.contactmusic.com/new/xmlfeed.nsf/mndwebpages/shakira%20is%20loveliest%20latina.

Chapter 6: Taking Chances and Making a Difference

33. Quoted in Laura Emerick, "Shakira's Instincts Lead Her All over the Musical Map," *Chicago Sun-Times*, June 5, 2005.
34. Quoted in Contactmusic.com, April 6, 2004, from Shakira press release. www.contactmusic.com/new/xmlfeed.nsf/mndwebpages/neurotic%20shakira%20will%20shock%20fans.
35. Quoted in Contactmusic.com, April 26, 2005, from Shakira press release. www.contactmusic.com/new/xmlfeed.nsf/mndwebpages/shakira%20makes%20mtv%20history%20with%20comeback%20video.
36. Quoted in Celebrityspider.com, "Shakira Angers *American Idol* Producers," April 7, 2006, www.celebrityspider.com/news/april06/article040606-19.html.

37. Quoted from Unite for Children Unite Against AIDS commercial, April 17, 2006, www.unicef.org/aids/index_33406.html.
38. Quoted from Unite for Children Unite Against AIDS commercial.
39. Quoted in *USA Today*, "Shakira, Karolina Win Humanitarian Awards," April 4, 2006, www.usatoday.com/life/people/2006-04-04-shakira-kurkova_x.htm.

Important Dates

1977

Shakira Isabel Mebarak Ripoll is born on Wednesday, February 2, to William Mebarak Chadid and Nidia del Carmen Ripoll Torado in Barranquilla, Colombia.

1991

Shakira releases her debut album, *Magia* (Magic).

1994

Shakira begins her acting career on the set of *El Oasis*; wins *TV y Novelas* magazine's Best Rear End contest.

1995

Shakira releases *Pies Descalzos* (Bare Feet); begins her tour for the album; Luis Fernando Ochoa becomes her producer.

1996

Columbia Records rereleases *Pies Descalzos* internationally.

1997

Pies Descalzos wins *Billboard* magazine's award for best new album; Shakira leaves *El Oasis*; Emilio Estefan Jr. becomes her manager and producer.

1998

Shakira is named Latin female artist of the year at the World Music Awards; *¿Dónde Están los Ladrones?* is released.

2000

Shakira begins her *Tour Anfibo* (Amphibious Tour); an album of the event, *MTV Unplugged*, is released and becomes her third straight platinum album; Shakira is invited to perform at the very first Latin Grammy Awards ceremony; Freddy DeMann becomes Shakira's manager.

2001

Shakira releases *Laundry Service*; Pepsi hires Shakira for their biggest commercial campaign since they hired Michael Jackson.

2002

Shakira moves to the United States with her fiancé, Antonio de la Ruá; appears on VH1's *Divas Las Vegas* special; appears on Dick Clark's *Primetime Rockin' New Year's Eve*.

2003

Shakira is named the youngest Goodwill Ambassador by UNICEF; begins her *Tour de la Mongosta* (Tour of the Mongoose); is named Loveliest Latin Lady by *Stuff* magazine.

2005

Shakira releases *Fijación Oral, Vol. 1* (Oral Fixation, Vol. 1) and *Oral Fixation, Vol. 2*.

2006

Shakira performs at the NRJ Music Awards in Cannes, France; receives the Best International Song Award for the song "La Tortura;" receives a Grammy Award for *Fijación Oral, Vol. 1*; appears on *American Idol* with Wyclef Jean.

For More Information

Books

Ximena Diego, *Shakira: Woman Full of Grace*. New York: Simon & Schuster, 2001. A good biography that follows Shakira's life from beginning to right before the release of *Laundry Service*.

Hal Leonard Corporation, *Shakira: Laundry Service*. Milwaukee, WI: Hal Leonard Corporation, 2002. Details the making of Shakira's album, *Laundry Service*, written by staffers and reviewers at Cherry Lane Magazines/Hal Leonard Corporation.

Hal Leonard Corporation, *Shakira: Oral Fixation*. Milwaukee, WI: Hal Leonard Corporation, 2006. Details the making of Shakira's albums *Fijación Oral, Vol. 1* and *Oral Fixation, Vol. 2*, written by staffers and reviewers at Cherry Lane Magazines/Hal Leonard Corporation.

Web Sites

Abstracts (www.abstracts.net). This Web site contains entertainment news and links to news about Shakira and other celebrities.

Entertainment Tonight (etonline.com). *Entertainment Tonight*'s Web site for celebrity news and interviews with Shakira and other celebrities.

Eonline (www.eonline.com). Contains celebrity news and gossip.

MTV (www.mtv.com). Contains biographies and articles about Shakira and other celebrities.

Rolling Stone Magazine (Rollingstone.com). The Web site for the famous rock magazine. Contains many full-length interviews with Shakira and other musicians, as well as CD reviews and tour information.

Shakira (www.shakira.com). Shakira's official Web site for news, biography, and tour dates.

in Bogotá with Shakira, 27
in Florida, 60, 62
reading and, 16
Shakira as child performer and,
11, 20–22

Sanz, Alejandro, 78
September 11,2001 terrorist
attack, 53
Seraphic Fire choir, 80
Shaki, 15
Shakira
on acting, 27
appearance of, 57
awards and honors received by,
21, 27, 35, 41, 46, 74, 79,
83, 85, 89
birth of, 15
characteristics of, 13–14, 18,
20, 76
childhood of, 10–11, 16, 18,
20–22
crossover appeal of, 12, 41
death phobia of, 20
education of, 16, 18, 25
on fight for control of music,
30–31
friends of, 12, 31, 39, 42
influences on music of, 29
lack of privacy for, 60
love of performing live, 66–67
on Madonna, 68
naming of, 15
on need for frequent new
records, 75
popularity of, 29, 32, 36, 64,
71, 79–80, 85
as representative of Colombia,
35

robbed, 41, 52–53
on Ruá, 45, 58
on self-acceptance, 57
siblings of, 12, 16, 35, 36, 60,
62
on technology in music, 40
on *Tour of the Mongoose,* 67
on war, 68
soap operas, 27–28, 36
Sony Columbia records
creative control and, 25–26,
29–30
Emilio Estefan, Jr. and,
40–41
Laundry Service and, 54
signed with, 12, 22, 25
Sosa, Mercedes, 42
Spirit of Hope Award, 85
Stevenson, Robert Louis, 16
Stuff (magazine), 74
"Suerte," 56

Tedeschi, Pablo, 25
television
appearances in Colombia, 21,
27–28, 36
appearances in United States,
45–46, 64, 79, 85–86
Téllez, Patricia, 28
Time (magazine), 63
Tonino (brother)
move to Florida, 12, 60, 62
as tour manager, 35, 36
"Tortura, La" ("The Torture,"
music video), 78–79, 83, 85
Tour Anfibo (Amphibious Tour),
42, 45–46
Tour de la Mongosta (Tour of the
Mongoose), 67, 71

Cover: © Reuters/CORBIS
AP Images, 11, 13, 19, 23, 24, 34, 37, 38, 49, 55, 61, 65, 66, 77, 81, 82, 84
© Stephanie Cardinale/CORBIS, 33
© Gary Hershorn/Reuters/CORBIS, 87
© Tim Mosenfelder/CORBIS, 69
© Daniel Munoz/Reuters/CORBIS, 47
© Reuters/CORBIS, 28, 48, 52
© Frank Trapper/CORBIS, 42
Carlos Alvarez/Getty Images, 17
Maurico Duenos/AFP/Getty Images, 88
Mark Mainz/Getty Images, 59
Baltazar Mesa/AFP/Getty Images, 43
Jeff Vespa/Wireimage.com, 70

Holly Day has written about music for over a thousand publications internationally, including *Computer Music Journal*, *ROCKRGRL*, *Music Alive!*, *Guitar One*, *Brutarian*, *Interface Technology*, and *Mixdown*. Over the past two decades, her writing has received an Isaac Asimov Award, a National Magazine Award, and two Midwest Writer's Grants. Her previous books include *The Insider's Guide to the Twin Cities* (3rd, 4th, and 5th editions) and *Music Theory for Dummies*.